Living Theology in India

Christian Heritage Rediscovered

The Series, as the name suggests, is meant to focus on Christian Faith & Living vis-à-vis topics like Literature & Poetry, Indigenous Philosophizing, Ethical response towards Agriculture, Health & Healing, Science & Technology, Ecofeminist Theology, Sociological approach towards Human Rights, Law & Politics, Arts, History of Ideas, Ancient Civilizations, Cultural Contiguity, Religious Cosmologies & Mysticism, Footsteps of famous Theologians, World Peace & Harmony, Global Capitalism, Network Marketing, Cybertheology, Population & Demographics, Epigraphic Studies, Contextualized Education, and many others. We welcome a Mss. on any topic/s mentioned, whether they are original works, scholarly monographs, collections of conference papers, revised dissertations, or translations of historical documents. Through the Series we, the Publishers, are striving to put forward published works that may help Institutions, Academic Bodies, Researchers, Scholars and the World at large in furthering their respective knowledge and understanding on the concerned subject. We welcome your comments on our efforts and further suggestions on how we can foster the upcoming thoughtful theologically grounded books.

Christian Heritage Rediscovered - 23

Living Theology in India

Stanley Jones' Contribution Towards Inter-Religious Dialogue

Rev. Zadingluaia Chinzah

CWI
Christian World Imprints™

First Published in 2015 by

Christian World Imprints(TM)
Christian Publishing & Books from India
H-12 Bali Nagar, **New Delhi-110015**
info@christianworldimprints.com
www.ChristianWorldImprints.com
Phone: +91 11 25465925

ISBN-13: 978-93-5148-079-2 ISBN-10: 93-5148-079-8

Cataloging in Publication Data--DK

Courtesy: D.K. Agencies (P) Ltd. <docinfo@dkagencies.com>

Chinzah, Zadingluaia, 1982- **author.**
Living theology in India : Stanley Jones' contribution towards inter-religious dialogue / Rev. Zadingluaia Chinzah.
pages cm. -- (Christian heritage rediscovered ; 23)
Includes bibliographical references (pages) and index.
ISBN 9789351480792
ISBN 9351480798

1. Jones, E. Stanley (Eli Stanley), 1884-1973. 2. Missionaries--India--Biography. 3. Missions--India. 4. Christianity and other religions--India. I. Title. II. Series: Christian heritage rediscovered ; 23.

DDC 266.76092 23

Printed at Replika Press Pvt. Ltd.

Dedicated to
my lovely daughters,
Faith and Grace

Foreword

One of the joys of being a teacher is to witness and wonder at the blossoming of bright-eyed, young theological students, embodying optimism, hope, and boundless potential, into public theologians, perhaps a little older but with the spark undiminished – public theologians who make noteworthy contributions at a variety of levels to life in the church and wider society, and continue to build the worldwide network of relationships through faithful ministry and ongoing publications. It is with this joy that I welcome Chinzah's contribution to Indian Christian Theology through this book which takes a fresh look at the ongoing vitality of E. Stanley Jones' Christology and how the life, legacy, teachings, challenges, and contributions of this wonderfully complex individual can continue to be heard on "the Indian road."

Let me continue on a personal note, reflecting on my own "Indian road" and using the account of the Transfiguration of Jesus: My instruction and initiation into pastoral status came rather early in my first pastoral placement. I was quite young, fresh out of seminary, and more than a little apprehensive at being out amongst the poor Dalits in India's villages. The members of the Pastorate Committee, had been very supportive and encouraging, and were prepared to give this untested product a fair chance. I was with another pastor, who by then had had the benefit of a couple of years' experience, and we were in the town nearby when in the distance I saw Devasundaram

Anna approaching. He was the eldest son of AnandAppa, the one who at the turn of the 19th and 20th centuries, had led his people out of the neighboring state in the midst of a devastating and debilitating famine, to settle down near Gauribidanur, Karnataka, where he and his clan of Indian Christians had been "discovered" by a wandering missionary, already worshipping in a hut, which was the first thing that they had built. AnandAppa had gone on to have sixteen children, nearly all of whom continued to live in the village with their families. I had a note book in which I had not only been writing my sermons, but also trying to sort out the tangled web of relationships that marked every person in my first congregation. Devansundaram Anna, was a long-standing church elder, and as he approached I said "Namaste, Devasundaram Anna", to which my colleague said, "Why are you greeting him? Those people should first greet you – you are their pastor", a rather unforgettable initiation into pastoral privilege and the perception that we were a special breed of people.

Privilege, prestige, pomp – something to which we're all entitled, right? I've been following quite a lot of threads in various Facebook posts about what the clerical collar does; appropriate and inappropriate ways of addressing the pastor; questions of leadership in missional congregations; and what the priesthood of believers really means. I'm not saying that all these discussion threads are about privilege, prestige, and pomp, no – rather they reveal to me the reality that certain questions remain on the radar and keep circling back with a lot of intensity time and time again.

In revalorizing E. Stanley Jones, we have to accept the ongoing challenges of this preacher, teacher, practitioner, ashram founder, tireless champion of India's poor and of Indian independence, and articulate speaker of truth to power, and truth to the powerless. He writes: "Again and again I felt no one has a right to teach others who is not learning from them. I came to India with everything to teach and nothing to learn. I now stay to learn as well, and I am a better man for having come into contact with the gentle heart of the East." (Quoted in Richard W. Taylor, *The Contribution of E. Stanley Jones*, Confessing the Faith in India, No. 3 (Madras: C.L. S., 1973), p. 76).

For Jones, the centrality of listening to Jesus involved the recognition that "We, therefore, do not come as an enemy to anything good, true or beautiful in any religion, in any race, in any culture." (Ibid., p. 108) This had to be lived out in practice, especially as goodness, truth, or beauty was not part of how aspects of religious traditions had dealt with those deemed "untouchable" and "depressed." Given this, the solution, listening to Jesus, sounds easy. But is it? We are caught up in the moment and dazzled by so many of the external realities of the time. We are caught up in the moment and mired in the messiness of everyday life. We are caught up in the moment and want that to continue so that we can bask in the glow and experience the afterglow. Do we take time to "listen to him?" God takes time for us and so it is that the moment passes – the light fades, the hopes of privilege, prestige, pomp are almost becoming a memory. And then, there's an invitation not only to the disciples then, but an invitation to us here and now. An invitation to recognize Jesus, his message, his call, and his challenge to be his companions and friends, in the midst of religious realities, hopes, promises, and challenges in India today.

There is much to be afraid of – the signs of the times are not propitious. All around us we hear about wars and rumors of war; the economic situation is poised on a knife's edge and we don't know what direction the economy will take; patterns of human relationship are becoming frayed and there is tension in every family; uncertainty clouds our imagination and insecurity has become the new normal; there are major upheavals in society, with huge questions regarding immigration, debt reform, health care, and what has been called the 'clash of civilizations.' It is in this context that we have to contend again with the words of Jesus, "Do not be afraid." In this context it is sobering to listen to Jones: "It has not all been sweetness and light. There have been failures in spirit and technique and outcome. Often it has been a painfully inadequate attempt to express the overwhelming vision." (Ibid., p. 97).

To return to the realities of India: The opulence of many wedding dinners has caught the attention of visitors and local people alike in a distinct way. It is indeed the moment when privilege, pomp, and prestige are on full display. Even among those who can't afford it, money flows like water, because they have to keep up appearances. In addition, many wedding invitations have the phrase, "please attend with family and friends." So much for careful counting and numbering the seats and informing the caterers and calculating the right number of beverages that will be consumed! Many of us take such invitations seriously and attend the wedding of perfect strangers! As the associate pastor of the large, urban, Hudson Memorial Church in Bangalore, my second posting after serving rural communities, I was invited to very many wedding feasts held at the Hudson Community Center, an asset owned by the church, which provided us with a significant income, since it was busy nearly every day of the year, used primarily for holding wedding feasts for people from all religious backgrounds. Our Muslim friends were made especially welcome since they hired the center for three full days! The facility was divided into various sections – the large hall, where the reception was held and several dining areas, including sections for vegetarians and non-vegetarians. There was another part where very few people ventured, beyond the kitchen, where the plates and dishes were washed. In going there in the course of wedding feasts, my wife and I, time and again, encountered people from the nearby slum, ragged, sitting on the floor, scrubbing the vessels in greasy water, people hired for that night, furtively and quickly eating the left-over food that uncaring guests had left on their plate. Contrasts and contradictions – just attend a wedding in India!

Jones writes, "My capacity to blunder led me to Christ." (Ibid., p. 74) These are powerful words indeed and it is in this context that the Gospel jolts us out of our complacency and reminds us about the good news of God – the good news that is not dependent on laws and rules and regulations, and human ways of upholding prestige, pomp, and privilege. Along with the disciples, we find ourselves on a mountain top where the transfiguration is now fading into a distant memory. But wait, the transfiguration is never over; the voice has not stopped speaking; the invitation to not be afraid is still valid. It's valid here and now, where we are invited to a table – a table set up on the way side, a table set up as a journey is underway, a table set up where the shadow of the cross falls – a table on the road where the host himself is the meal; where the transfiguration takes place every time the holy communion is celebrated; where the body and blood signifies, and indeed is, the real presence of our living and loving Savior right among us here and now; a meal that is breathtaking in its extravagance; indiscriminate in its welcome; stupefying in its recklessness of saying "poof" to our self-gratifying notions of pomp, privilege, and prestige, and instead proclaiming, even as we walk along the Indian road, thatall are welcome to walk along with us, ahead of us, beside us, behind us, pilgrims and fellow-seekers welcome to eat together as we journey on the way.

- **Rev. Dr. J. Jayakiran Sebastian**
Dean of the Seminary and
H. George Anderson Professor of Mission and Cultures
The Lutheran Theological Seminary at Philadelphia
Philadelphia, PA, USA

Easter 2015

Acknowledgements

Researches and publications of any work is seldom the endeavour of an individual. This is true in the case of this book. However, the importance of the intent and content of doing a research, it is the people behind all the tussles that make it more significant and successful.

There have been many significant people that helped in materialising this work. First of all, I cannot mention the immensity of gratitude and possibility I owe to my Church, the Lairam Jesus Christ Baptist Church, for giving me the widest possible opportunity. I am thankful to Rev. Dr. O. V. Jathanna, Rev. Dr. J. Sebastian, Rev. Dr. David Joy, Rev. Dr. Sham P Thomas, Rev. Dr. D. J. Muthunayagom my theological mentors at the United Theological College. Also, special thanks to Rev. Dr. Elizabeth Koepping, Dr. Brian Stanley, Dr, Jack Thompson my mentors at the University of Edinburgh, and to Dr. Robin Boyd, for his advice.

Words fall short to express my gratefulness to my parents, Rev. Hrangzuala and Zirmawii for their support, prayers and belief.

The spaces and pages within this book will never suffice to contain the contributions of my beloved wife Rebecca Lalhmangaihzuali.

- Zadingluaia Chinzah
Lawngtlai
2015

Contents

Chapter 1

Introduction

Explorations of Christology in India may be mapped along two dominant trajectories:

a) in which the contributors are themselves Indian, comprising both Christians and Hindus;
b) the missionaries who had been deeply involved toward constructing a Christology deemed relevant for India.

Eli Stanley Jones falls in the latter trajectory. Taking into consideration the history of modern India, particularly with the cultural and intellectual renaissance in Bengal in the wake of orientalism, Raja Ram Mohan Roy's *Precept of Jesus* initiated the first of many other explorations in the person and work of Christ in India. With serious thought being given to this branch of theology, there have been debates and responses. In each of the attempts at constructing Christology in India there have been marked differences and shifts. It is within such context that Eli Stanley Jones' Christology expressed in the oft-mentioned phrase, "Christ of the Indian Road" makes a significant contribution to Indian Christian theology.

Eli Stanley Jones (1884-1973), an American Methodist had a distinct approach for his missionary work in India. His concern was the 'Indianization' and 'De-westernization' of the Indian Christians. The "Christ of the Indian Road" is how Stanley Jones believes Christ can be understood in India. His "Christ of the Indian Road" does not stem from an academic interpretation of what an Indian Christ can be interpreted, but rather how Christ can be naturalized in the Indian setting. His "Christ of the Indian Road" was therefore a result of his varied missionary experiences in India. It is an attempt at unfolding Stanley Jones' "Christ of the Indian Road" for discovering the possibilities of Indian attraction towards Christ in an era where the Christian community was apparently seen as anti-nationalistic towards the Indian nationalistic movement. It was within this movement, in the political, religious and social movements spearheaded by Mahatma Gandhi who fervently raised issues with which missionaries came to grips that Stanley Jones' "Christ of the Indian Road" came to be renowned. The importance of analysing Stanley Jones' "Christ of the Indian Road" within the theological setting in India is to assess its consequences and results.

Stanley Jones' "Christ of the Indian Road" also plays a prominent part in his initiated Round Table Conferences with people of other faiths. The extent of acceptance in these conferences is an important consideration of Stanley Jones' "Christ of the Indian Road". The presentation of Christ in such conferences added another dimension to Jones' "Christ of the Indian Road" resulting in the difference of approach and inculturation amidst the wider explorations of Christology in India. This study will thus attempt to bring out the contribution of Stanley Jones' "Christ of the Indian Road" to Indian Christian theology.

Stanley Jones' "Christ of the Indian Road," was not an attempt at constructing a new Christology in India amidst the existing explorations. His was an earnest quest of putting into practice the meaning and nature of Christ, and how Christ can be interpreted in Indian understanding. This quest however became a noteworthy shift in the way Christ was understood and contextualised through academic articulation by theologians before his time.

The study of Indian theology has been occupied and controlled by elitist and sanskritic explorations of Christology, giving little space to possibilities of developing a people oriented Christology. Hence, Christology in India, in spite of the emergence of liberation theology is still in the grasp of few academics dominating the field. It is within such a context that people like Stanley Jones becomes important.

The purpose set before this study can therefore be put into two objectives:

a) to highlight the importance of a people oriented Christology. This form of Christology will assume that for Christ to be fully explored, it needs to reach out the mass. Stanley Jones' "Christ of the Indian Road" is such a Christology. It reaches out to the everyday experience of the masses and it critically responds to the elitist and academic explorations of Christ. Hence, it marks a shift within the wider exploration of Christology in India. It endeavours to highlight the central message of Jones' "Christ of the Indian Road" and how he naturalises Christ to the Indian mind. In attempting thus, it will attempt to look how this Christ was portrayed and examine the intention of deriving such an approach.
b) it will attempt to analyse the subsequent contribution of Jones' "Christ of the Indian Road" to Indian Christian theology by finding possibilities of its influence. This will attempt to respond to a pertinent question: Did Stanley Jones' "Christ of the Indian Road" have an impact on Indian theology? Thus, in attempting to tackle the issue placed in front of the proposed study, it will enable one to assess the relevance of Stanley Jones for Indian theology today.

The study will be an analysis of the writings of Eli Stanley Jones particularly those related to the field chosen. It will also attempt to consult written sources on Stanley Jones by various other writers. The research will be based on both primary and secondary printed sources.

A critical appraisal of Stanley Jones' "Christ of the Indian Road" will be endeavoured by giving particular attention to the historical context in which the "Christ of the Indian Road" was initiated. In an attempt to highlight the distinctiveness of Stanley Jones' "Christ of the Indian Road" as a contribution to Indian Christian Theology, the following two methods of study will be taken into consideration;

a) an analysis of the "Christ of the Indian Road" will be undertaken, taking in serious consideration the context of Christianity in pre-indepedence India, the Indian Nationalist movement, Jones' acquaintance with Mahatma Gandhi and the latter's attack on missionaries and Christian mission.
b) it will look into Stanley Jones' "Christ of the Indian Road," a construct of experience in the midst of the wider Indian Christological explorations articulated academically through Sanskritic terms. Hence, these methods of studies will be used to construe a critical appraisal of Stanley Jones' "Christ of the Indian Road".

This book will have for its main focus the study of E Stanley Jones' "Christ of the Indian Road". It will endeavour to look into the method in which Jones contextualises Christology. This book will comprise analysis of the nature and form of Stanley Jones' Christology. It will attempt to deal on the central message of Stanley Jones' "Christ of the Indian Road" conveyed to the Indian mass. It will endeavour to look into the possibilities that relate the gospel of Jesus Christ to the cultural realities of the Indian people. An examination of Stanley Jones' "Christ of the Indian Road", which was developed through experience in the light of Jones' presentation of Christ in the religious Round Table Conferences with people of other faiths, will be endeavoured. It is not however an attempt at reviewing Jones' book with the same title.

However, this book be limited to certain aspects of Stanley Jones' thought and writings, hence an emphasising on his "Christ of the Indian Road". Due to the limitation of the requirements of the author, the wider theological thoughts and contributions of Stanley Jones, especially his exposition of the Kingdom of God and Conversion, will not be dealt with extensively. However, cross-examination with these thoughts will be attempted when required.

The difficulty in assessing the impact of Jones arises at two levels, viz., the absence of sufficient acknowledgment of his works particularly within the Indian theological circles, and, the lack of contemporary research dealing with Jones' thought. These problems have been raised both by Stephen Graham, who asserts the absence of academic research undertaken of Jones,[1] and David Bundy. Bundy raises his case with two distinct remarks:

> The myth of Jones as missionary revolutionary statesman, charismatic preacher, best-selling author, and spiritual giant remains unexamined. Perhaps because of his superhuman image, Jones has been the subject of very little critical reflection and research. Study has been hampered by lack of access to paper and records of Jones.[2]

Bundy nears accuracy of such interpretation in his analysis since research on Stanley Jones after Bundy's piece in 1988, there has not be a major work done except two publications by Stephen Graham and one by Paul A. J. Martin, with scattered research at master's level.[3]

---

1 Stephen A. Graham, *Ordinary Man, Extraordinary Mission*: *The Life and Work of E. Stanley Jones* (Nashville: Abingdon Press, 2005), 392. Hereafter, Graham, *Ordinary Man.*

2 David Bundy, "The Theology if the Kingdom of God in E. Stanley Jones," in *Wesleyan Theological Journal,* Vol. 23, No. 1 (Spring, 1988), 58.

3 Stephen Graham has written *The Totalitarian Kingdom of God: The Political Philosophy of E. Stanley Jones* (University Press of America, 1998) and, *Ordinary Man, Extraordinary Mission: The Life and Work of E. Stanley Jones* (Abingdon Press, 2005). Paul Martin's work, *Missionary of the Indian Road: A Theology Stanley Jones* (Theological Book Trust, 1996) is a publication of his doctoral research at the Cambridge University.

Chapter 2

The Centrality of the Christ of Experience in the Life and Thought of Eli Stanley Jones

A Hindu writer, in expressing his attitude toward Christian missionaries remarked:

> The missionary is the representative of a society, a polity, a social system, a religion and a code of morality which are totality different from our own. He comes as a belligerent and attacks our time honoured customs and institutions, our sacred literature and traditions, our historical memories and associations...He wishes to destroy our society, history and civilization.[4]

This attitude represents a remarkable majority of approaches towards Christian missions and missionaries in 19th and early

4 Quoted in J. N. Farquhar, *The Crown of Hinduism* (London: Oxford University Press, 1913), 33.

20th century India. In fact, this attitude is one of the reasons why Christian missions in India are connected with imperialism. In such a context, it is remarkable that Eli Stanley Jones, a missionary could again acceptance and recognition from the Indian voices. When awarded the Gandhi Peace Prize, a spokesman of the government of India called him the greatest interpreter of Indian affairs during that time.[5] This chapter attempts to highlight a brief biographical detail of Stanley Jones. It will look into the theological formation of this 'best known Anglo-Saxon missionary'[6] which propelled him in the centre of Indian Nationalism and Christian missions.

To recognize the importance of Christ and Experience in the theology of Stanley Jones, it is vital to discern the influential factors that contributed to such a formulation. To recognise such factors, it is necessary to examine stages, events and persons in the life of Jones.

The Life of Eli Stanley Jones

Eli Stanley Jones was born in Clarksville, Maryland on the 3rd of January, 1884[7] exactly a century after founding Methodist Episcopal Church in America. Being brought up in the Methodist tradition, Jones was introduced to the Church through the Sunday school from an early age. Jones' second contact with the Church was in his 15th year when he listened to a preacher from John Bunyan's Church in England. It was at this occasion that Jones first decided to accept Christ, a decision which did not last. Jones recalls this event as a 'half-conversion which was a whole failure'.[8] Jones' 'real' conversion occurred in his 17th year, in an evangelistic meeting organised by the Methodist evangelist, Robert J. Bateman. Bateman, a converted

5 Richard W Taylor, "E. Stanley Jones 1884-1973: Following the Christ of the Indian Road" in Gerald H. Anderson, Robert T. Coote, Norman A. Horner and James M. Phillips (Eds.), *Mission Legacies: Biographical Studies of Leaders of the Modern Missionary Movement* (Maryknoll: Orbis Books, 1994), 339.

6 David Bundy, "The Theology of the Kingdom of God in E. Stanley Jones", 58.

7 Graham, *Ordinary Man*, 21.

8 E. Stanley Jones, *Songs of Ascents: A Spiritual Autobiography* (Nashville: Abingdon Press, 1968), 27. Hereafter, Jones, *Ascents*.

alcoholic, was filled with a fiery passion for God[9], a character that remarkably influenced Jones. The sermons of Bateman led to the discovery of Jones' 'whole future packed' into Christ. It was through Bateman that Jones received Christ, and experienced the conversion which was the principal theme of American Methodist preaching.[10] Hence, the revivalist tradition of the Methodist, especially through Robert J. Bateman played a dominant role in introducing Christ as the centre of Jones' life, drawing him nearer to God and changing his life forever. In the wake of his conversion, Jones was assisted through prayer and counselling by Miss Nellie Logan, his school teacher. She took him, in Jones' words to the 'Holy of Holies'. She was the person Jones' mother entrusted him to, and Jones without any qualms remarks, 'I adore Christ; I reverence Miss Nellie.'[11] Miss Nellie continued to be an important spiritual strength in Jones' life and ministry. In fact, Jones owed his grounding in conservative theology to Miss Nellie.[12] The Methodists' tradition of revivalist preaching, evangelism and personal experience, in addition to the pietistic nature of Miss Nellie, were the formative factors that prepared and moulded Jones' theology.

Stanley Jones and the Asbury Experience

When Jones entered Asbury College in Wilmore, Kentucky, an institution of the Methodist Church, Jones was already licensed as a local preacher by the Methodist Episcopal Church.[13] Apart from his course study comprising Greek, Caesar, Rhetoric, Butler's Analogy, Church History and Ralston's Element of Divinity,[14] Jones

---

9 Jones, *Ascents*, 27.

10 John L. Peters, *Christian Perfection and American Methodism* (Nashville: Abingdon Press, 1956), 98. Methodism in America grew rapidly through revivalist preaching and evangelism. See also, Leonard Woolsey Bacon, *A History of American Christianity* (New York: Christian Literature Company, 1897), 198-206.

11 Jones, *Ascents*, 44.

12 Paul A.J. Martin, *Missionary of the Indian Road: A Theology of Stanley Jones* (Bangalore: Theological Book Trust, 1996), 41. Hereafter, Martin, *Missionary*.

13 Graham, *Ordinary Man,* 23.

14 Graham, *Ordinary Man,* 28.

was deeply involved in evangelistic work in addition to preaching 'nearly every Sunday at college.' During his stay at Asbury, Jones continued preaching and in some cases involved saving people.[15] Jones' preaching activities during his studies at Asbury gave him the zeal for evangelism.

Jones' second year at Asbury involved him with the Holiness Movement. In fact, his early evangelistic works was deeply influenced by the Holiness Movement.[16] The Movement's spiritual and intellectual father, John Wesley insisted the religious experience of conversion and Christian perfection,[17] traits which can be found in Jones. Asbury college itself was committed to foreign missions and evangelism as it was to the promotion of piety, sanctification and holiness.

However, the most important contribution the college made to Jones' theology was its typical Methodist insistence on 'experience'.[18] It was through this 'experience', Jones later recalls, that his call to mission field was born,[19] though the direct basis of his call to Africa was his involvement with the Student Volunteer Movement (SVM). The SVM, concerned for revival and mission,[20] introduced a new direction in the life of Jones. The SVM gave strong emphasis on the authority of the Scripture, prayer and Holy Spirit,[21] a belief and practice which he always carried within him. The subsequent call to mission after joining the SVM, Jones recalls, was the biggest thing that came out of his religious experience.[22] Hence, it was through

---

15 Graham, *Ordinary Man,* 38.

16 For a study on the Holiness Movement, see Melvin E. Dieter, T*he Holiness Revival of the Nineteenth Century* (Lanham: The Scarecrow Press, 1996).

17 Vinson Synan, *The Holiness-Pentecostal Movement in the United States* (Grand Rapids: Wm B. Eerdmans, 1971), 13-14.

18 Jones, *Ascents,* 67.

19 Jones, *Ascents,* 71.

20 Paul E. Pierson, "The Student Volunteer Movement for Foreign Missions (SVM)" in A. Scott Moreau (Ed.), *Evangelical Dictionary of World Missions* (Grand Rapids: Baker Books, 2000), 914.

21 Pierson, "The Student Volunteer Movement", 914.

22 Jones, *Ascents,* 71.

the SVM that Jones career as a missionary began. Instead of sending Jones to Africa, the Methodist Board sent him to India.

Stanley Jones and the Indian Experience

To assess the centrality of the Christ of experience in Stanley Jones' theology, it is important to acknowledge and examine the presence and work of Jones in India and how the Indian mission influenced and developed his thoughts. In doing so, a brief description of the American Methodist mission in India will suffice. The Missionary Society of the Methodist Episcopal Church in 1852 set aside a sum of $7,500 to launch the Indian mission.[23] The real work was undertaken by William Butler who arrived at Bareilly, the birthplace of Indian Methodism in December 1856.[24] From 1856 onwards the Indian Methodist Mission had been working towards three important fields; healing, teaching and preaching; or, to be precise in the fields of medicine, education and evangelism.[25] In 1908, a year after Jones' arrival, there were 200,000 Methodists in India and by 1914, they were the second largest Protestant Church in India.[26] Majority of the converts were from the low caste groups and the untouchables, and baptism was carried *en masse*.[27]

Stanley Jones was 23 years of age when he first began his work as a missionary in India. He spent four years as a Pastor of Lalbagh Methodist Church in Lucknow. Stanley recalls that being a Pastor to Church made up of Anglo-Indians, English, Americans and English-speaking Indians made him feel he was not in the centre of India but

---

23 James K. Mathews, *South of the Himalayas: One Hundred Years of Methodism in India and Pakistan* (Nashville: Editorial Department, Board of Missions of the Methodist Church, 1955), 79.

24 Mathews, *South of the Himalayas*, 80.

25 For fuller details of the work of Methodist Mission in India see Mathews, *South of the Himalayas*, 95-148. See also J. Tremayne Copplestone, *The Methodist Episcopal Church, 1896-1939*/Vol. IV: Twentieth Century Perspectives (New York: Board of Global Ministries and United Methodist Church, 1973), 777-859.

26 Martin, *Missionary*, 47.

27 Martin, *Missionary*, 47.

at the edge of it.[28] He married Mabel Lossing, a Methodist missionary teaching at Isabella Thoburn College in Lucknow, in 1911; and in the same year was moved to Sitapur, 50 miles from Lucknow to become the District Superintendent for the American Methodist Mission.[29] At Sitapur, Mabel looked after the boys' school and Stanley Jones was the district missionary working six months among the Indians and six months with the English speaking congregation.

Taking charge as the district superintendent of the Methodist mission in Lucknow laid out stressful work for Jones. Few years later three other districts were added under his charge in addition to being made the Agent of the Lucknow Publishing House which involved editing the *Indian Witness*, the Church's weekly paper.[30] The colossal task set under his charge, though undertaken with great passion, had its consequence on his health. Coupled with his health problem was the frequent nervous collapses that made him return to America even though his furlough was still a year away. After a year's break, Jones returned to India and the nervous collapses continued to recur. It was after his return to India, recalls Jones that he had to take regular visits to the mountains to recuperate.[31] His physical illness left him during a prayer in Central Methodist Church in Lucknow.[32] This incident led to the centrality of Christ in the life and ministry of Stanley Jones.

Stanley Jones found something amiss in his missionary endeavours as he remarks:

> After eight years continuously in India in various types of missionary work ranging from pastor of an English church, head of a publishing house, missionary to the villages, district superintendent of large areas, I felt strangely drawn to work among the educated high castes, the intelligentsia. As a mission we were doing very little indeed among them.

28 Jones, *Ascents*, 82.

29 Martin, *Missionary*, 41.

30 Martin, *Missionary*, 48.

31 Jones, *Ascents*, 89.

32 Jones, *Ascents*, 89.

> We had taken the line of least resistance and nearly all our work was among the low castes.[33]

It opened a new possibility of his work in India, to be an evangelist to the intellectual class. Jones mentions that the key person in India is 'the man [sic] who thinks', and that in changing their mind, one also changes the minds of the people down the line to the lower class".[34] Hence in 1920, Jones was appointed by the Mission Board as the unprecedented evangelist to educated Indians.[35] Assuming his new responsibility, Jones travelled throughout India and very soon became nationally famous as a preacher which later propelled him to international recognition. This led to the organising of the Round Table Conferences, being the responsive discussion with people of other faiths which also resulted in Jones speaking in Temples and in a particular case, the Arya Samaj College.[36]

Stanley Jones soon found himself gradually leaning towards the struggle for India's independence spearheaded by Mohandas Gandhi. The years of his involvement with Indian nationalism in general and Mohandas Gandhi became one of the most important phase of his life and thought. Jones became, in M. M. Thomas' interpretation, 'the foremost in understanding and interpreting Gandhi sympathetically from within the orthodoxy of the Christian Church'.[37] Jones himself admits to being intimately associated with the struggle taking place in India that he was denied a visa in 1944.[38] During his acquaintanceship with Gandhi, Jones spent much of his time in Sabarmati ashram which also led to Jones staring his own

---

33 E. Stanley Jones, *The Christ of the Indian Road* (London: Hodder and Stoughton, 1925), 27-28. Hereafter, Jones, *Indian Road.*

34 As quoted in Graham, *Ordinary Man,* 111.

35 Martin, *Missionary*, 41.

36 Jones, *Ascents,* 113.

37 M. M. Thomas, *The Acknowledged Christ of the Indian Renaissance* (London: SCM Press, 1969), 225.

38 E. Stanley Jones, *Mahatma Gandhi: An Interpretation* (Nashville: Abingdon-Cokesbury Press, 1948), 6. Hereafter, Jones, *Gandhi.*

ashram. In 1930, Jones started his own ashram at Sat Tal, an ashram with Gandhian style.[39]

Stanley Jones and Mohandas Gandhi

Stanley Jones met Mohandas Gandhi in 1919 when Jones gave an address at St. Stephen's College, Delhi[40] and in 1923 at Poona Hospital after Gandhi was released from his imprisonment.[41] Jones then became among the important circle of Gandhi's Christian friends. Gandhi became the model of the spiritual Kingdom of which Jones had been preaching and passionate about. On Gandhi, Jones remarks:

> I am still an evangelist. I bow to Mahatma Gandhi, but I kneel at the feet of Christ and give him my full and final allegiance. And yet a little man, who fought a system in the framework of which I stand, has taught me more of the spirit of Christ than perhaps any other man in East or West.[42]

He even goes to the extent of saying about Gandhi's death, 'never did a death more fittingly crown a life, save only one-that of the son of God.'[43] Among the various reasons which attracted Jones to Gandhi was Gandhi's Christ-likeness, which Jones mentions repeatedly in his writings. Jones looked upon Gandhi as a holy man.

In analysing the written works of Jones, it can be sensed that his theological exposition is not academic in the strict sense. In fact, in his writings he failed to mention sources or acknowledge them. But there are traces where the origin of thoughts may be discerned. Most of his work and theology are derived from his personal experience, both events and people. This resulted in the distinctiveness of

---

39 Taylor, "E. Stanley Jones 1884-1973", 343.

40 Jones, *Ascents*, 131.

41 E. Stanley Jones, *Along the Indian Road* (New York: Abingdon Press, 1939), 124. Hereafter, Jones, *Along*.

42 Jones, *Gandhi*, 8.

43 Jones, *Gandhi*, 41.

Stanley Jones approach towards mission and evangelism, from other American Methodist missionaries of his time or those before him. His desire and objective to evangelise the intellectual class of India sets him apart from his Methodist predecessors and contemporaries. This objective transformed his mission and also its impact which was dissimilar to the previous engagement of the Indian Methodist mission which had success among the lower class of India.

Chapter 3

Stanley Jones, Mohandas Gandhi and Indian Nationalism

The collusion between mission and colonialism in India from the late 19th century to the 20th century has been a major issue. This issue became an undeniable problem especially during the years that saw the emergence of Mohandas Karamchand Gandhi and Indian nationalism. Among the obvious reasons for such an attitude was the fact that both missionaries and colonizers spoke the same language, and that both mission and colonization were two parts of western expansion.[44]

The inherent indifference to, and withdrawal of Indian Christians from the political struggle for independence was gradually becoming a formal procedure. Hence, the Indians who converted to Christianity were condemned as deserters of ancestral religion, betrayer of customs, traditions, modes of life, and were seen to 'ape' European manners, totally losing their identity as people of a distinct

44 Sigfrid Deminger, *Evangelist pa Indiska Villkor: Stanley Jones och den Indiska Renassansen 1918-1930* (Orebro: Bokforlaget Libris, 1985), 194. Hereafter, Deminger, *Evangelist.*

human civilization.[45] In addition, there were widespread instances that reinforced such attitudes. Christian missions enjoying political protection of the British rule, financial help in philanthropic and educational work were visible especially during 1840-65.[46] Later, there were cases of Governors and high ranking officials of the British Empire openly announcing their support of missions.[47] Moreover, the efforts to evangelise college students increased from the turn of the 20th century.[48]

The present chapter will attempt at highlighting the prominence of the issue mentioned above by analysing Gandhi's attitude towards Christianity in India, and his role in Indian nationalism. It will also endeavour to locate Stanley Jones within such context, to discuss his position, and highlight how it relates to his thought and work.

Mohandas Gandhi on Christianity and Indian Nationalism

Mohandas Gandhi arrived on the scene of Indian nationalism after his success in South Africa. He was a Moderate in his non-violent approach towards the British administration, yet an Extremist in his demand for a *Hind Swaraj* - Home rule for India. Political retaliation was not the only agenda Gandhi produced before the British rulers; he wanted to do away with every form of imperialism, i.e., cultural, religious as well as economic imperialism.[49] In pursuit of these goals Gandhi adopted a policy of Non-cooperation. Fisher remarks:

> Non-co-operation became the name of an epoch in the life of India and of Gandhi, and that it was negative enough to be peaceful but positive enough to be effective. It entailed

45 C. F. Andrews, *The Renaissance in India: Its Missionary Impact* (Edinburgh: Foreign Mission Committee of the Church of Scotland, 1912), 165.

46 A. I. Mayhew, "The Christian Ethic and India" in L.S.S. O'Malley (ed.), *Modern India and the West: A Study of the Interaction of their Civilizations* (London: Oxford University Press, 1941), 319-320.

47 Mayhew, "The Christian Ethic and India," 320.

48 Deminger, *Evangelist*, 193.

49 Martin, *Missionary*, 6.

> denial, renunciation and self-discipline. It was training for self-rule'.[50]

Gandhi's main charge against British rule in India was that it led to economic oppression,[51] and that it rendered India more helpless than she ever was, politically and economically.[52] Gandhi believed that by achieving self-government, the people of India would not be forced to accept slavery or serfdom.[53] The major task was to purify India; England's expulsion would come as a by-product. Therefore, Indians would non-co-operate non-violently.[54] Having introduced Gandhi and locating him within Indian nationalism, attention will be given to his attitude towards Christianity.

To analyse and examine the issues raised by Gandhi regarding Christianity, it is essential to acknowledge that for Gandhi, religion meant participation in politics, and that every activity is determined by one's religious outlook.[55] This understanding explains the attachment of religious ideas in Gandhi's political philosophy. Politics, for Gandhi, is of little value without religion.[56] His religious ideals and beliefs therefore can be seen in his political ideals. Gandhi remarks:

> For me, politics bereft of religion are absolute dirt, ever to be shunned. Politics concern nations and that which concerns the welfare of nations must be one of the concerns of a man (sic) who is religiously inclined, in other words, a

---

50 Luis Fisher, *The Life of Mahatma Gandhi* (London: Jonathan Cape, 1951), 208-209.

51 S. Radhakrishnan (ed.), *Mahatma Gandhi: Essays and Reflections on his Life and Work* (London: George Allen & Unwin, 1939), 23.

52 Shriman Narayan (ed.), *The Selected Works of Mahatma Gandhi*, Vol. VI (Ahmedabad: Navajivan Publishing House, 1968), 21.

53 Glyn Richards, *The Philosophy of Gandhi: A Study of his Basic Ideas* (London: Curzon Press, 1982), 148.

54 Fisher, *Life of Mahatma Gandhi*, 218.

55 Richards, *Philosophy of Gandhi*, 135.

56 Richards, *Philosophy of Gandhi*, 136.

> seeker after God and Truth...Therefore, in politics also we have to establish the Kingdom of Heaven.[57]

Gandhi's tryst with Christianity did not begin in an affirmative tone. From an early age, Gandhi had an embedded prejudice about Christians, portrayed by missionaries, creating an early dislike for a religious teaching he held with utmost respect later on in life. He recounts of such an instance:

> In those days, Christian missionaries used to stand in a corner near the high school and hold forth, pouring abuse on Hindus and their gods. I could not endure this. I must have stood there to hear them once only, but that was enough to dissuade me from repeating the experiment...I also heard that the new convert had already begun abusing the religion of his ancestors, their custom and their country...it created in me a dislike for Christianity.[58]

To aggravate his dislike for Christianity, Gandhi's later contacts in England and South Africa were with evangelical Christians filled with the objective of converting him to Christianity. The issue of conversion thus became a central issue in Gandhi's discussion on and about Christianity and Christian missions. Gandhi viewed conversion as a form of religious imperialism and an instrument of denationalisation.[59] Gandhi was a proponent of religious harmony, and as such was not tolerant of one religion trying to overshadow the other. For Gandhi, the different religions are beautiful flowers from the same garden, or they are branches of the same majestic tree.[60] After Gandhi's address to a missionary conference in Madras, Bishop Whitehead remarked that above anything else 'he [Gandhi] was opposed on principle to all proselytizing on the part of the

57 Narayan (ed.), *Selected Works of Mahatma Gandhi*, Vol. VI, 435.

58 Shriman Narayan (ed.), *The Selected Works of Mahatma Gandhi*, Vol. I (Ahmedabad: Navajivan Publishing House, 1968), 21.

59 Martin, *Missionary*, 7.

60 Margareth Chatterjee, *Gandhi's Religious Thought* (London: MacMillan Press, 1983), 53.

missionary.'[61] Gandhi particularly addressed the Indian converts who had gone to the extent of adopting western lifestyles and completely forgetting their ancestral religion and faith. His early experiences with Christianity in differing context led him to conclude that Christianity became disfigured when it went to the West.[62] The competition and opposition between different churches and denominations was one of the reasons Christianity was disfigured in the west, he said.[63] He attributed the aggressive and proselytizing nature of Christianity to European modification, a feature he found conflicting with the teaching of Jesus.[64] In addition to his stance against the western form of Christianity, Gandhi was as Bishop Whitehead commented, the representative of an extreme form of modern reaction against western influence and western civilization in India.[65]

However, though he was much against western Christianity, Gandhi had an immense respect for Christ and the Gospel. Commenting on the influence of the Gospel message on Gandhi, Mayhew comments, 'his vivid sense of sin, his faith in human nature when inspired by love, his recognition of the value of the human vicarious suffering, show strong evidence of Gospel meditation.'[66] In fact, his non-co-operation on non-violent lines was influenced by the teachings of the Sermon on the Mount.

Stanley Jones and Indian Nationalism

There were few missionaries that rose to national prominence and during the political, religious and social unrest spearheaded by Gandhi. Stanley Jones was among such few missionaries. Frykenberg, in selecting such missionaries known for their explicit sympathy for Indian nationalism and anti-imperialistic attitudes, remarks:

---

61 Henry Whitehead, *Indian Problems in Religion Education Politics* (London: Constable & Co., 1924), 233.

62 Narayan (ed.), *Selected Works of Mahatma Gandhi*, Vol. VI, 87.

63 K. L. Sheshagiri Rao, *Mahatma Gandhi and Comparative Religion* (Delhi: Motilal Banarsidass, 1978), 29.

64 Rao, *Mahatma Gandhi and Comparative Religion*, 29.

65 Whitehead, *Indian Problems*, 233.

66 Mayhew, "The Christian Ethic and India," 316.

> Such missionaries as Allan Hume (American Marathi Mission, who was one of the founders of Indian National Congress) and Charles F. Andrews (SPG Cambridge Mission to Delhi), as well as Verrier Elwin, J.N. Farquhar, E. Stanley Jones, Edward Thompson, and Amy Carmichael, were among the more prominent.[67]

Among the prominent missionaries, Charles F. Andrews was the most prominent, and was also among the closest friends of Gandhi. Jones comes second only to CF Andrews in this regard. In fact, as Stephen Graham notes, Stanley Jones' thought became radically different from 1919, the moment Jones came into contact with Gandhi.[68]

The beginning of political involvement for Jones simultaneously came with his decision to evangelise the educated class of the Indian mass. He was not only sympathetic towards the Indian struggle for self-rule but was a proponent of such ideals. He was, in the early phase of his involvement in Indian politics, favourable to the demands of the moderate nationalists. The demands were along the lines of Montague Declaration which agreed more representation from the Indians, gradually leading towards self-government.[69] Jones' moderate political stance is visible from his negative response to Gandhi's proposals against the government through Satyagraha. Jones felt the policy of Gandhi was too violent and radical and hence requested Gandhi not to begin with his non-violent civil disobedience.[70] The unexpected turn in Jones' political stand took place when Gandhi defended Satyagraha as a political application of Christ's words. Though Jones was still sceptical of Gandhi's boycott of foreign goods and the non-cooperation that

---

67 Robert Eric Frykenberg, "Christians in India: An Historical Overview of their Complex Origins" in Robert Eric Frykenberg (Ed.), *Christians and Missionaries in India: Cross Cultural Communication since 1500 with Special Reference to Caste, Conversion, and Colonialism* (Cambridge: William B Eerdmans, 2003), 60.

68 Graham, *Extraordinary Man*, 142.

69 http://www.storyofpakistan.com/articletext.asp?artid=A120

70 Jones, *Gandhi*, 134.

went ahead, by 1923 Jones was convinced of what he described as a 'decidedly Christian' element in Indian politics, and was openly welcoming the new force of Indian nationalism.[71] The change in Jones' political position can be discerned when he remarked that he wanted to 'see India politically free'.[72] In addition to his claim as a pacifist, Jones asserts:

> I am also interested in India's freedom. I believe it to be the birthright of every nation to express itself in self-government. I believe it will be good for India and Britain when the right is conceded and implemented.[73]

Moreover, Stanley Jones had also realised from his evangelistic work among the educated and intellectual elite the broader social and political issues of Christian missions being understood as agents of imperialism.[74] His closeness to Gandhi was also with the objective of convincing Gandhi to Christianity.[75] Moreover, the personality of Gandhi and his practical usage of the Sermon on the Mount in his political deliberations enabled Jones to see an opportunity that could enhance his efforts of evangelising the intelligentsia since Gandhi had already directed India's attention to Christ.[76] Hence, Jones' new political position, his evangelism among the educated class and his close relationship with Gandhi became inseparable objective for Jones' evangelistic work in India.

The quest for an understanding of Jones' political position is discernable in his message to Indian Christians and to missionaries. From his involvement both in missions and Indian politics, Jones was aware of the attitude many Indian Christians and missionaries had towards the Indian struggle for self-government albeit the missionaries mentioned above. He remarks that in 1923, the Church

---

71 Martin, *Missionary*, 58.

72 Jones, *Indian Road*, 53.

73 E. Stanley Jones, "My Position Restated" in *The Indian Witness*, 11th April, 1940, 233.

74 Graham, *Extraordinary Man,* 150.

75 Graham, *Extraordinary Man,* 150.

76 Martin, *Missionary*, 59.

was 'facing' Indian nationalism – aloof, afraid, semi-hostile, or at least with deep questioning, and that the dawn has arrived for Indian Christians to partake in nation building, that Indian Christianity is part and parcel of India – her India's future her future.[77] His message to the Indian Christians was 'that they get in touch with Indian national aspirations, study India's national needs and get ready to shape the India of tomorrow,'[78] and that they commit themselves wholeheartedly to Indian independence.[79] Elsewhere he also comments:

> Now no movement will succeed in India at the present time that does not ally itself with the growing national spirit of India. We Christian missionaries must learn that lesson. We must see to it that Indian Christians are not un-Indianised. This does not refer to dress and eating. They will be modified more or less by Christian and non-Christian. These things do not count. What is essential is that Indian Christians remain at heart Indians. That they get in touch with Indian National aspirations, study India's national needs and get ready to have a hand in the shaping of the India of tomorrow. Political Indian will desperately need the steadying hand of Christian ideals.[80]

Jones sought greater identification with national ideals and his Christian message by founding an ashram, an Indian institution revived in the 20th century by Gandhi and Rabindranath Tagore.[81] Ashrams are attempts to reclaim an ancient Indian social institution for contemporary, often nationalist, social, political, or religious purposes.[82] Jones' ashram, known as Sat Tal, had the same element

77 E. Stanley Jones, "Opportunities for the Indian Church Facing Indian Nationalism" in *The Indian Witness*, August 1, 1946, 1.

78 Martin, *Missionary*, 165.

79 E. Stanley Jones, "Opportunities for the Indian Church Facing Indian Nationalism II" in *The Indian Witness*, August 15, 1946, 1.

80 As quoted in Deminger, *Evangelist*, 57.

81 Martin, Missionary, 167.

82 Taylor, "E. Stanley Jones", 342.

with the additional objective of evangelism. The importance of Sat Tal was Jones' commendable identification of the need for an Indian expression and interpretation of the Gospel. The evangelistic objective of the ashram being recognised, it is also necessary to accept that Sat Tal aimed at encouraging nationalistic feeling among Christians in India. Jones' use of homespun khaddar cloth was in itself a symbol of nationalist movement and his continuing involvement in Indian nationalism.[83] Sat Tal's distinctiveness from other ashrams in existence was that it revolved around Christ,[84] without being exclusively Christian in membership. Defending his ashram as being clearly the opposite of syncretism, Jones remarked that Sat Tal was indeed an attempt at interpreting Christ in Indian terms.[85]

83 Taylor, "E. Stanley Jones", 343.

84 Jones, *Ascents*, 221.

85 Martin, *Missionary*, 180.

Chapter 4

Stanley Jones' Pursuit of the "Christ of the Indian Road"

In attempting to draw out Stanley Jones' Christology, as expressed in his oft-mentioned phrase 'Christ of the Indian Road', it is of utmost importance to acknowledge and analyse his missionary approach towards the Indian mass. This approach precursors the 'Christ of the Indian Road', Jones' Christ-centred message to the Indian mind. He enumerates his approach thus:

> a) Be absolutely frank; b) Announce beforehand that there is to be no attack on anyone's religion; c) Allow them to ask questions at the close; d) Get the leading non-Christians of the city where the meetings are held to become chairmen; e) Christianity must be defined as Christ, not the Old Testament, not the West, not even the system build around him in the west, but Christ himself and to be Christian is to follow him; and f) Christ must be interpreted in

> terms of Christian experience rather than through mere argument.[86]

Jones' approach proceeds from his realisation of two principles: one, the need for an alternative to the existing missionary approaches of his time, and two, the importance of Christ within the Indian struggle for self-rule. Jones further added that Christ must be placed in an Indian setting, must be the Christ of the Indian Road.[87] His Christology is therefore bereft of traditional Christianity, in the particular sense of doing away with doctrinal and theological deliberations, but instead the introduction of a disentangled Christ – disentangled from being bound up with western culture and western forms of Christianity.[88]

In exploring Jones' concept of the 'Christ of the Indian Road' however, the attempt is not to conduct a review of his work by the same title, but a discussion of the idea that led to his interest in and objective of evangelising the intellectual mass of India, and the subsequent inspiration behind his writing of the book *Christ of the Indian Road.* It must also be acknowledged that the Christ of the Indian Road played the central role in the Round Table Conferences initiated by Jones. The focus will be to interpret the content of Jones' Christology, and endeavour to highlight the features that became acceptable to Indians despite their tendency to identify Christianity with imperialism.

The objective of this chapter is twofold; one, to highlight the implication of the Indian Road as a theme in Jones' Christology; and two, to analyse the content of Jones' Christology, the Christ of the Indian Road.

The Indian Road as a Theme

The 'Indian Road' plays a central role in Jones' Christology. It represents, in Martin's words, 'his [Jones'] conscious efforts to take the Indian context into account in his thinking and work'.[89]

---

86 Jones, *Indian Road*, 32-33.

87 Jones, *Indian Road*, 33.

88 Jones, *Ascents*, 110.

89 Martin, *Missionary*, 163.

The Indian Road is a paradox of two opposing realities in terms of geographical and physical features, materials and philosophy. It is a conflict of varied existence. It is the daily walk of life, from its grass-root intricacies to lofty ideas that run through the length and breadth of India. This paradox is India - fascinating, alluring and paradoxical India.[90]

Jones' analysis of the Indian Road as a paradox begins with the historical facts where the Indian Road had been marred by various invasions in its early past. He accepts that the formation of the culture of the Indian Road was shaped and influenced by the intermingling of various races. He relates four ideas about God and human beings in the Indian Road: the Unity of all things, Karma, Transmigration, and Caste.[91] Jones also comments on the vast and comprehensive all-inclusive Hinduism. Among the various characteristics of the Indian Road, the prevalence of God-consciousness or God-hunger captures Jones' thought the most. The Indian Road at this level simply means India, the country to which he was sent as a missionary.

The second level of the Indian Road was its implication for a form of faith which could be interpreted in Indian expressions. At this level, the Indian Road becomes a call for Indians to look at the Gospel through an Indian prism. Jones' rationale was the indigenisation of the Gospel message. For this endeavour, Jones looks at the ways in which the authors of the Gospels and St. Paul expressed Christ in differing forms and expression.[92] Jones further analyses the history of Christianity in Europe to highlight the fact that what became of Christianity in Europe was the result of its transformation through Greek thought and Roman law. Jones also claims that medieval Europe implanted Anglo-Saxon tendencies in Christianity which were never before present[93] and more controversially that Protestantism was the result of European influence upon Christianity. Jones therefore raises a pertinent issue regarding such tendencies in

---

90 Jones, *Along*, 12.

91 Jones, *Along*, 13.

92 E. Stanley Jones, "Influence of the Indian Heritage upon Christianity" in Richard W. Taylor, *The Contribution of E. Stanley Jones* (Madras: CLS, 1973), 41.

93 Jones, "Influence of the Indian Heritage upon Christianity," 43.

Christianity by his suggestion of adopting Indian tendencies within Christianity. The Indian Road at this level is hence Jones' attempt at influencing Christianity with Indian heritage. He finds the Indian form of Ashram a worthy inheritance for Christianity. He even goes to the extent of saying that the Indian heritage in Christianity would be the richest in its history, second only to the Jewish heritage.[94]

The task of this inheritance rests on the shoulders of the Indian church and the Indian Christians. Jones opines that as long as the Indian church does not remain Indian, she will not be able to contribute to Christian theology. Jones suggests that the adoption of the Indian spirit of god-searching would contribute a great deal to Christianity if Christianity were to be made Indian, it would not be rejected as western forms of Christianity currently are. On this task, Jones remarks:

> In order to do that the Indian must remain Indian. He must stand in the stream of India's culture and life and let the force of that stream go through his soul so that the expression of his Christianity will be essentially Eastern and not Western. This does not mean that Indian Christianity will be denied what is best in Western thought and life, for when firmly planted on its own soil it can than lift its antennae to the heavens and catch the voices of the world. But it must be particular before it can be universal.[95]

Jones' Pursuit of the Christ of the Indian Road

To analyse and emphasize the content of Christ of the Indian Road, it is pertinent to enquire the reasons for Jones' adoption and advocacy of such a Christology. Having discussed earlier the prevalent attitudes towards Christianity and Christian missions in India, it is evident that these attitude also changed the approach of Jones, a Christian missionary from the west. Jones explored possibilities in which he could evangelise without being connoted with imperial motives. Jones discovered his alternative in the person of Jesus Christ and his message. At this point, it can be safely assumed that the

94 Jones, "Influence of the Indian Heritage upon Christianity," 44.

95 Jones, *Indian Road*, 231.

allegations mentioned above worked to Jones' advantage in two basic ways. The first way was that it compelled Jones to adopt an approach which identified itself with India, her people and her nationalistic aspirations. Secondly, his message came to be surprisingly acceptable for those Jones addressed because imperialism and dominance were not part of it. This is evident from his message which addresses the importance of Christ and not the desire to dominate.[96]

Jones' first step of approach was the distinction he made between Christ and Christianity. Jones wanted to show that there were possibilities for the Indian to accept and follow Christ without the negation of their nationalistic aspirations.[97] Hence, Jones' Christology became a response to the previously mentioned allegations because the Christ presented was not tainted with westernization, and was an alternative because it placed religious experience at a significant level of importance. That the presented Christ stood in judgment on Christian nations was skilfully portrayed.

Jones' commendable recognition of the change in the Indian intellectual thought towards Christian missions, and the subsequent use of Christ's teaching by Gandhi laid the groundwork for the formation and development of his Christology. His visits to the ashrams of both Gandhi and Tagore in Sabarmati and Shatineketan respectively, brought a realisation that Christian ashrams were an alternative by which the missionary message could be conveyed without being foreign, that it was a way in which missionaries could identify themselves with the national movement. Jones believed that the ashram could be truly Christian and truly Indian,[98] and in fact he founded the Sat Tal ashram along this line. Having thus established himself as a supporter and sympathiser of Indian nationalism, Jones began to draw an attitude by which his message of Christ could be heard and accepted in India. He remarks:

> I felt that we who come from a foreign land should have the inward feeling, if not the outward sign, of being adopted

96 E. Stanley Jones, "Christian Missions Not Domination, not Denomination, but Christ" in *The Indian Witness*, April 3, 1934, 2.

97 Martin, *Missionary*, 79.

98 Taylor, "E. Stanley Jones 1884-1973," 343.

> sons of India, and we should offer our message as a homage to our adopted land; respect should characterise our every attitude; India should be home, her future our future, and we her servants for Jesus' sake. We have come, then, this far in our thinking: that the Christ of the Indian Road, with all the fullness of meaning that we can put into those words, should be our message to India.[99]

Hence, Jones' Christology can be approached and understood from his use of the Christ of experience and his presentation of the Christ of the Indian Road, which 'naturalises' Christ in an Indian setting.

The Christ of Experience

Having established himself as an adopted son of India, Jones began his evangelistic work and began preaching about Christ among the intellectual elite. Although the audiences addressed were the intellectual elite, Jones' goal was not an academic exploration of Christology. The main content of his Christology was 'the Christ of experience,' the beginning of the idea which was given to him by a Hindu,[100] and which was also an important part of his Methodist upbringing. It came out of a situation where Jones was inquiring about the reception Christ would have received in India, had Christ come disassociated from westernisation. It was a Hindu, the mayor of an unnamed city who raised the question of what it meant by finding Christ.[101] Jones response to this enquiry laid the foundation by which he could preach his experiences of Christ, experienced through conversion. The significance of experience, an outcome of Jones' Methodist and Asbury upbringing is visible in his insistence on 'interpretation of Christ through experience and not argument'.[102]

The inquiry of the Hindu mentioned and the subsequent response to it led to the development of the Round Table Conferences

99 Jones, *Indian Road*, 35.

100 E. Stanley Jones, *Christ at the Round Table* (London: Hodder and Stoughton, 1928), 19. Hereafter, Jones, *Round Table.*

101 Jones, *Round Table*, 19.

102 Jones, *Indian Road*, 33.

with an approach which had, in Jones' words, 'three outstanding things in it; Experimentation, Verification and Sharing of Results'.[103] Jones decides the use of scientific approach because he felt that all those gathered in the Round Table Conferences were men who had in some way or the other experimented religion as a working hypothesis of life. It was a very formal approach as this approach would look into the various findings, the members had in religious experiences and share those experiences. Thus, began the regular Round Table Conferences where men of influence and education gathered to discuss about their experiences, and to listen to Jones' testimony of how he was transformed by Christ. Jones was thus able to realise the objective he set for himself during his college days, to be a witness. It was by being a witness that Christ came to be accepted and listened to in India, especially by the Hindus.[104]

Remarkable in Jones' approach and among the reasons for the acceptance of the 'Christ of experience' was his knowledge of Hindu religion and spirituality. This knowledge came from his study of Hinduism in which Mahatma's role in influence is detectable. Jones recalls his first meeting with Gandhi who subsequently advised him to 'study the non-Christian religions more sympathetically to find the good that is within them, in order to have a more sympathetic approach'.[105] Hence, it was not futile for Jones to align his approach in such ways. It was through an understanding of the religious mindset of the Hindus especially that Jones was able to portray Christ as the way through which God is found. This impresses the inner soul of the Hindus whose religious life is aimed at the finding and realising of God. The Christ of experience conveyed the message that it was the expression of the 'real self' and that the Christ of experience is an offer not a demand.[106] The reception of the Christ of experience was that those present in the Round Table Conference could feel that Christ was central in the discussion, that he was the master not by loud arguments but from doing things for human life.[107] Hence, the

103 Jones, *Round Table*, 21.

104 Martin, *Missionary*, 85.

105 Jones, *Gandhi*, 70.

106 Jones, *Round Table*, 136.

107 Jones, *Round Table*, 55.

'Christ of Experience' was able to walk the Indian Road fully aware of what lay before, behind and besides.

Presenting the Christ of the Indian Road

It is in analyzing the content of the Christ of the Indian Road that the importance of Gandhi for Stanley Jones surfaces. The importance is the Christ-likeness character in Gandhi's love for his people. Christ-likeness as a character comes from Gandhi's self-sacrifice for his people. This self-sacrificial act is explained through the centrality of the Cross which is the sum total of Christ's sacrifice. This raises the question of the consequence of Christ's death on the Cross for those believing in him, and concerns the subsequent appropriateness of 'naturalising' it for the Indian mind in Jones' exploration of the Christ of the Indian Road.

Stanley Jones' distinctive message of the Cross becomes visible through his attempt at interpreting atonement by indianising it. In explaining the importance of understanding the Cross, Jones remarks that, it lead to the understanding of Christ which lead to an understanding of God; and, an understanding of God ultimately leads to the understanding the meaning of the universe and life[108], the search of the Indian mind. Hence, atonement becomes the central message of his Christology, atonement understood in the specific term of attunement, an idea given to him by a Hindu youth.[109] He explicates attunement as being attuned to the nature of God. Jones in this way presents Christ as the harbinger of harmony and peace between God and created beings.[110] The Christ of the Indian Road harmonizes three levels of disharmony that exist in human beings' relationship with their spiritual environment, i.e., disharmony within oneself, with other beings and with God. At the first level of disharmony that erupts between the higher self which 'craves goodness, nobleness, God' and the lower self which 'craves and conceives evil'.[111] Secondly, the disharmony with other beings within

108 Jones, *Round Table*, 230.

109 Jones, *Indian Road*, 234.

110 Jones, "Influence of the Indian Heritage upon Christianity", 53.

111 Jones, *Round Table*, 231.

society which bread jealousies, petty quarrels, court wrangling, family feuds, wars, distinction of class and caste.[112] Finally, in the third level is the lack of harmony or correspondence with the highest and most important portion of the spiritual environment, God.[113] The harmony and peace through Christ, in Jones' presentation leads to at-one-ment, overcoming the three levels of disharmony. For Jones, this is the meaning of the Cross, the sacrifice which attuned us to God. Jones did not talk directly about sin, though his explanation of disharmony is the closest he gets to doing so. This rendering of Jesus Christ as saviour is different from the classical Christian presentation of the atonement. The message of the Christ of the Indian Road therefore, comprises forgiveness, sacrifice, and harmony embodied in atonement through the Cross. Jones' Christ of the Indian Road, thus incorporated Indian spiritual heritage and the Christ of experience.

Jones' concern was for a 'naturalised' Christ who would be a part of the national life of an Indian and contribute its power to India's uplift. Jones remarks that the followers of this Christ 'need not change their dress, their diet, their names – they can stand in the stream of India's culture and life and interpret Christ from that standpoint rather than stand in western culture.[114] Jones believed that naturalising Christ in India would have a result which would stand in contrast to the existing 'mission compound mentality' where the followers of Christ were segregated from the Indian way of life. He also strongly advocated naturalisation for he felt that it was only when India accepted Christ as the untrammelled and disentangled Christ that she could contribute to Christian theology.[115]

The central idea of Jones' Indian Christ is that Christ should be untrammelled by western thought and accents. Jones explicates a mental picture of the Christ of the Indian Road using an imagined conversation between his friend and a Brahmin;

> 'Then how do you like the Christ of the Indian Road?' The Brahman thought a moment, mentally picturing Christ of

112 Jones, *Round Table*, 231-232.

113 Jones, *Round Table*, 232.

114 Jones, *Along*, 136.

115 Jones, "Influence of the Indian Heritage Upon Christianity," 46.

> the Indian Road – he saw him dressed in Sadhu's garments, seated by the wayside with the crowds about him, putting his hands upon the hands of the poor, unclean lepers who fell at his feet, announcing the tidings of the Kingdom to stricken folks, staggering up a lone hill with broken heart and dying upon a wayside cross for men, but rising triumphantly and walking on that road again.[116]

Jones' Christ of the Indian Road understands the toils, pains and sorrow of the Indian mass by entering into their lives and by being with them. The Christ here is not different from the Christ of the gospels except for his sadhu's garb. The presented Christ is simple and humble, elements which could capture the heart of the Indian mass.

116 Jones, *Indian Road*, 39-40.

Chapter 5

Impact of Stanley Jones in India

Locating both Stanley Jones and his message within the context of the socio-political and religious movement in India enables an assessment of his impact and contribution to Indian Christian theology particularly in the light of what was achieved or what remained to be achieved. An assessment of an impact of an American missionary to a remarkably dissimilar socio-political and religious situation in India, as particularly attempted in this study has to take into account his achievements, influences and the way in which the person is remembered within the field of work chosen, in this case within the theological circle in India.

Jones' wider contributions have been dealt by Stephen Graham,[117] who considered Jones' general impact in the West, and by Paul A. J. Martin who looks at Jones' contribution to missiology as a result of the issues raised by Gandhi discussed in the earlier chapters.[118] The particularities involved in assessing Jones' impact

117 Graham, *Ordinary Man,* 392-397.

118 Martin, *Missionary*, 227-238. In relation to Jones' contribution to missiology, see pp. 227-234 where Martin brings out Jones' contribution in seven summarized points.

in India require an examination of his Christology from different perspectives. His impact upon individuals has also been immense. Stanley Jones' impact upon the wider Indian Christian theology is an attempt which presupposes his influence and contribution towards Christology in particular.

Contributions of E. Stanley Jones to Indian Christian Theology

Jones' contribution to Indian Christian theology will be analysed at three levels as given in the following points.

a) Jones' contribution towards the study of a living theology in India;
b) Jones' influence upon different exponents of Indian Christian thought;
c) Jones' contribution towards inter-religious dialogue.

The given points overlap, correlate and complement each other as will be explored below. Before delving deeper into the attempted study, it is appropriate to remark that in studying Jones' Christology, indigenization, dialogue and the founding of the ashrams beginning at Sat Tal cannot be treated as distinct identities and themes. The main reason being that Jones' Christology comprises all the three mentioned, and that these themes are directions by which Jones attempts at amplifying and relating his Christology, insistently phrased 'Christ of the Indian Road'.

Jones' Contribution towards the Study of a Living Theology in India

The *Confessing the Faith in India* series, published by the Centre for the Study of Society and Religion (CISRS), Bangalore, consists of studies in the theology of prominent Indian Christian thinkers who have sought to express Christian faith against the background of Indian life and culture. In the preface to the series is given the rationale in which Christian thinkers for such series are chosen. The rationale requires that the thinkers portray a living theology which is valuable to the Indian Church which seeks to confess Christ in the context of the thought-forms and life situations of its own setting.[119] The rationale is drawn from a statement of the East Asia Christian Conference which says,

> A living theology must speak to the actual questions men in Asia are asking in the midst of their dilemmas; their hopes, aspirations and achievements; their doubts, despair and suffering. It must also speak in relation to the answers that are being given by Asian religions and philosophies, both in their classical form and in new forms created by the impact on them of western thought, secularism and science. Christian theology will fulfil its task in Asia only as the Asian churches, as servants of God's Word and revelation in Jesus Christ, speak to the Asian situation and from involvement in it.[120]

The first ten in the series are Christian thinkers in India, namely, Chenchiah, Chakkarai, Nehemiah Goreh, Kaj Baago, M. M. Thomas, S. K. George, A. G. Hogg, E. V. Mathew, Stanley Jones and Charles Freer Andrews. The series has two types of distinction, viz., Indian missionary Christian thinkers, and missionaries in India. Jones is one of the three non-Indian Christian thinkers to be considered for the important first ten of the series. Richard W. Taylor has done a brief and comprehensive introduction of Stanley Jones and his thought with selections of Jones' writing in the book titled, *The Contribution of E. Stanley Jones with Selection from his Writings*, in 1975. Richard Taylor was himself an American Methodist missionary to India and was involved with the CISRS from 1961.

In his book, Richard Taylor looks at the various aspect of Jones' thought. Although the intention of the series was neither a detailed biographical study nor a detailed study of Jones' contribution,[121] it was nonetheless, a study which looked at the major areas in which Jones made an impact in India in general. It introduced Stanley Jones

119 M.M. Thomas & T.K. Thomas, "Preface" in P. T. Thomas, *The Theology of Chakkarai with Selections from his Writings* (Bangalore: CISRS, 1968), iii-v.

120 Quoted in Thomas, *Theology of Chakkarai*, iii.

121 Taylor, *Contributions of E. Stanley Jones*, vii.

as a famed evangelist and preacher, both in India and America, with brief notes on his missionary activities within India and outside. In looking at the various aspect of Jones' work, Taylor deals with six fields of study in which Jones' influence in India can be seen, viz., The Indian Christ, Round Table Dialogue, Ashram, Concern for Social, Economic and Political Justice, Gandhi and the issue of conversion. In dealing with such themes, Taylor extensively deals with Jones' involvement in the founding and establishment of Ashrams in India and abroad. Taylor also mentions individuals who were in some ways or the other influenced by Jones.

The inclusion of Stanley Jones in such a series is in itself a contribution to Indian Christian theology. It also affirms that Jones' theology is a living theology that concerns the Indian Christians in their multi-faceted context. It also affirms Jones his place among the foremost gamut of Christian Protestant thinkers in India whose life and work need extensive analysis and appraisal.

Jones' Influence upon Different Exponents of Indian Christian Thought

One of those directly influence by Stanley Jones' Christ of the Indian Road was Chandran Devanesen (1917-1982). Chandran Devanesen was the first Indian principal of the Madras Christian College and also an ardent follower of Gandhian principles.[122] Jones' Christology had such an impact upon Devanesen that he wrote a poem with the same title in his book *The Infinite Christ.*[123] Devanesen's poem explicates practically and vividly the essence of Jones' Christology. His poem, 'Christ of the Indian Road' addresses in singularity individuals from every walk of life along the Indian Road. Devanesen poetically describes Christ of the Indian Road, thus:

> Listen to Him, O men and women of India,
> you and your children.
> The hands that are His
> will speed the plough through our fields of poverty.

122 http://www.mcc.edu.in/index.php?Itemid=56&id=30&option=com_content&task=view

123 Chandran Devanesen, *The Infinite Christ* (Madras: CLS, 1948), 24-26.

The minds that are His
will create the plan which hums
in the roar of the city,
which throbs in the rhythm of the tabla
beaten in the village.
The hearts that are His
will clear the way and build the
road that is gentle even to crippled feet.
Let Him lead us in the march of Humanity,
to a wonder that awaits,
to the eye-unseen, the ear-unheard Future
that leads over star-track and Beyond![124]

Jones envisages in his exploration of Christ of the Indian Road, that Indians should interpret Christ in their own understanding.[125] Devanesan's poetic interpretation of the Christ of the Indian Road fulfils what Jones' desires most of his Christology.

Dr. Eddy Asirvatham, who died on May 7, 1969, at the age of 72, was a theologian, political scientist and ardent nationalist. He was a member of the pioneering 'Rethinking Christianity' group in Madras. Political scientists all over India looked upon him as their guru.[126] Reminiscing on his days at Sat Tal ashram, Asirvatham declares that the most fruitful of his days was spent with Stanley Jones.[127] He further adds that the style of Christianity that influenced him as a form of life was derived from Jones.[128] At this juncture, it is appropriate to recall, as elsewhere mentioned, that for Jones, Christianity meant Christ. Thus, in Eddy Asirvatham, one finds the influence of Jones in Indian political theology.

One of the earliest forms of theological expressions in the history of Christianity is the expression through art. 'Art in Christian history began with the drawing of the fish as an expression of an

---

124 Devanesen, *Infinite Christ*, 26.

125 Jones, *Indian Road*, 254.

126 Described in the cover of Asirvatham's book, *The Evolution of my Social Thinking* (Madras: CLS, 1970).

127 Airvatham, *Evolution*, 29.

128 Airvatham, *Evolution*, 30.

irreplaceable confession of Jesus Christ', says Masao Takenaka.[129] The importance of Christian Art in India has been dealt by Richard Taylor[130] which is a noteworthy contribution to the study of Indian paintings of Christ.[131] Alfred D. Thomas is yet another example of Jones' influence. Thomas attempts to paint Christ in an India setting and in an Indian style,[132] and his early painting was 'Christ of the Indian Road,' an influence of Jones. Yet again Jones' desire that Indians should interpret Christ is found through the painted work of Thomas. Alfred D. Thomas is, in Fleming's view, a painter in whom the Indian church has at last found an artistic expression.[133] A description of his painting of the 'Christ of the Indian Road' reads:

> 'Christ is here represented holding a child in His arms, while the mother of the child kneels before Him offering a lotus. Around Him are grouped two dozen typical figures of the Indian road, men, women and children, one of them mounted on an ass, another leading sheep and lambs, while behind is a ruined wall disclosing in the background the tower of a Hindu temple. The central figure of Christ arrests the eyes: robed in purest white, the face marking a departure from the traditional likeness, the dark hair crowned with thorns and set off by a halo of pale gold..[134]

Apart from the above mentioned there are a number of individuals, strictly Christian intellectuals and not theologians, whose lives were influenced by Jones. Violet Paranjoti mentions

---

129 Masao Takenaka, *Christian Art in Asia* (Tokyo: Kyo Bun Kwan and CCA, 1975), 11.

130 Richard W. Taylor, *Jesus in Indian Paintings* (Madras: Christian Literature Society, 1975),

131 Masao Takenaka, "Review of Jesus in Indian Paintings by Richard W. Taylor" in *The Ecumenical Review*, Vol. 29, No. 1, January 1977, 102-103.

132 Richard W. Taylor, "Some Interpretations of Jesus in Indian Painting" in Saral K. Chatterjee (introduced.), *Acknowledging the Lordship of Christ: Selected Writings of Richard W. Taylor* (Delhi: ISPCK, 1992), 5.

133 Daniel Johnson Fleming, *Each with His Own Brush: Contemporary Christian Art in Asia and Africa* (Nashville: Friendship Press, 1938), 54.

134 Taylor, *Jesus in Indian Paintings*, 115-116.

individuals such as Judge Sawarkar, Mr. A. Noble Rajamani, Mr. C.S. Manickam, Miss Sarah Paul, Mr. Lemuel Patole, Mr. Sundrakumar, Mr. B.V. Canaran and Mr. S.P. Kelkar. 'These individuals', Paranjoti adds, 'are a miniature cross-section of Indian intelligentsia who have come into contact with Jones either personally or indirectly through his writings.'[135] Rajamani, the then editor of *The Christian Focus*, remarks:

> He [Jones] has met and known their [Hindu's] most representative men – from Gokhale to Gandhiji and Tilak to Tagore- and seen India through their eyes. In his ashram at Sat Tal, he has tried to recapture the life of meditation for which Indian rishis were famed, and he has been alongside the Indian people in their fight for freedom. From such knowledge and self-identification comes his power to interpret Christ to India. He has made Christ of Galilee the Christ of the Indian Road. He has restored the true Gospel image to the Europe-tainted Christ, so making Him acceptable to prejudiced minds.[136]

Jones' Contribution towards Inter-religious Dialogue

The most important impact of Jones as seen from the preceding chapter is Jones' initiation of dialogue with people of other faith in his oft mentioned Round Table Conferences (RTC). Of naming the meeting as the RTC, Jones does not mention it as a derivative of the political Round table Conferences between the Indian nationalists and the British Empire. The RTC began in 1926[137] from which it served as a concluding discussion on religious experience after the

---

135 Violet Paranjoti, *As Evangelist on the Indian Scene: Dr. E. Stanley Jones* (Bombay: Bombay Book & Tract Society, 1970), 105.

136 A. Noble Rajamani, "Mr. Evangelist" in Violet Paranjoti, *As Evangelist on the Indian Scene: Dr. E. Stanley Jones* (Bombay: Bombay Book & Tract Society, 1970), 109-112.

137 Paul A. J. Martin, "Walking the Indian Road: The Contribution of E. Stanley Jones to Missionary Theology in India" in *Collected Papers of North Atlantic Missiology Project and Currents in World Christianity Project 1996-2001* CD ROM, Position Paper Number 87.

public meetings held in halls and theatres of major cities of India. The RTC comprised a gathering of thirty to fifty leading men of the cities in which they met, with careful attention given to avoid an overcrowding of Christians over the other faiths in attendance. It also included representatives of other faiths who have been untouched by Western education and spoke only the vernacular languages.[138] The ratio of attendance of RTC, Jones remarks, was decided with two-thirds non-Christians and one-third Christians.[139]

Before delving into the core of this contribution, it is appropriate to mention that in dealing with Jones' Christology, his ashrams and dialogues cannot be treated as separate subjects as the objective behind the beginning of ashrams and the round table conferences was conveying the message of the Christ of the Indian Road. Thus, in speaking about his contribution towards Indian Christian theology in particular and theological studies in general, Jones' Christ of the Indian Road comprises identification, indigenisation and religious dialogue without which an assessment of it is incomplete.

The uniqueness of Jones' RTC was that they were experienced-based dialogue between men of different faiths with the absence of religious debate on truth or assertion of religious imperialism. To assess the contribution of Jones towards interreligious dialogue, attempt will be made highlighting in brief the writers of dialogue have said in regards to the aforementioned theme. Wesley Ariarajah, among the most prominent writers of this theme traces religious dialogue particularly in India to the meeting held in Nagpur in 1960.[140] Elsewhere, he also mentions that the concern for dialogue with people of other faiths originated at Edinburgh 1910, followed later at Jerusalem 1928, Tambaram 1938, to New Delhi 1961.[141] In both cases, Ariarajah mentions Paul David Devanandan as the pioneer of Interreligious dialogue. With the pertinence of the concern for

138 Jones, *Round Table*, 26.

139 Jones, *Ascents*, 237.

140 Wesley Ariarajah, *Hindus and Christians: A Century of Protestant Ecumenical Thought* (Grand Rapids, Michigan: Wm. B. Eerdmans, 1991), 128.

141 Wesley Ariarajah, "Interfaith Dialogue (Dialogue, Interfaith)" in Nicholas Lossky et. al (eds), *Dictionary of the Ecumenical Movement* (Geneva: WCC Publications, 2002), 312-313.

dialogue with people of other faiths, the World Council of Churches in 1968 engaged Stanley J. Samartha of India to pursue with greater intensity a study begun some years earlier on "The Word of God and the Living Faiths of Men".[142] This led to the creation of a sub-unit on dialogue within WCC with Samartha as the director.

Jones has clearly enumerated his desire as a missionary that the conferences and meetings he initiated were with the intellectuals of his time. The meetings were not about academic explorations, but a sharing of experiences. Yet, in all the meetings, Christ was never left unsaid. The various elements involved in the meetings mentioned are the concerns Stanley J. Samartha raised five decades later.[143] This suggests that Jones' RTC were pioneering efforts at interreligious dialogue although Wesley Ariarajah leaves him out when tracing the history of interreligious dialogue.

Jones' approach in his work as a missionary mentioned in the earlier chapter has 6 principles all dealing with attitudes towards people of other faiths. In fact, Jones rightly claims he felt the need for such dialogue with people of other faiths in India, forty years before the vogue of dialogue arose.[144] Thus, was initiated the Round Table Conference to serve such purposes. Jones recollects:

> I suggest that no one argue, no one talk abstractly, no one discuss the other person's faith pro or con, no one preach at us; but you simply tell what you have found in experience. If you are an agnostic or an atheist, tell us what your agnosticism or atheism has done for you in experience.[145]

The approach was not without the knowledge of the faiths of the people involved in the conferences. Jones' writings to a very large

---

142 Ariarajah, "Interfaith Dialogue (Dialogue, Interfaith)," 314.

143 The concerns raised by Samartha has been comprehensively summarized by Wesley Ariarajah. See S. Wesley Ariarajah, "Some Glimpses into the Theology of Dr. Stanley Samartha" in C.D. Jathanna (Ed.), *Dialogue in Community: Essays in Honour of S.J. Samartha* (Mangalore: Karnataka Theological Research Institute, 1982), 231-233.

144 Jones, *Ascents*, 236.

145 Jones, *Ascents*, 237.

extent reveal his knowledge of Hinduism particularly.[146] There are perhaps similarities in the approach and theology of Devanandan with that of Jones.

Paul David Devanandan (1901-1962) was one of the great Indian Christian theologians in the wake of independent India. Having completed his education both in India and the United States, he joined the faculty of the United Theological College, Bangalore in 1932 and taught philosophy and comparative religions. He was with the YMCA, and was an ordained presbyter of the Church of South India.[147]

The similarity of thought in Devanandan and Stanley Jones can be seen from their concerns for Christian involvement in national politics, that theology is a living interpretation, not just academic explorations and the concern for relations with people of different faiths. A striking similarity can be drawn from Jones' address and concern for Indian Christian's involvement in national politics mentioned elsewhere in this study to that of Devanandan's concern which says that the Christian must not only refrain from antinationalism, but should contribute in a positive way to the making of the nation and its plans.[148] It is believed that the name Devanandan was an addition to his Christian name Paul David with the sole objective of asserting his identity as an Indian.[149] It is evident from his writing that Devanandan understood the attitude towards Christianity in India which in many ways clarifies his national consciousness.[150] Devanandan in a similar attitude with Jones raised the issue that Christianity cannot only be expressed in Western terms,

---

146 See Jones, *Along*, chapter 3.

147 See, CISRS, *In Memory of Devanandan* (Bangalore: CISRS, 1962) for Devanandan's biography.

148 P. D. Devanandan, *Christian Concern in Hinduism* (Bangalore: CISRS, 1961), 86.

149 John C. England, et. al. (Ed.), *Asian Christian Theologies: A Research Guide to Authors, Movement, Sources*, Vol. I (New York: Orbis Books, 2002), 236.

150 P. D. Devanandan, "The India We Live In" in *Presenting Christ to India Today: Three Addresses and a Sermon delivered to the Synod of The Church of South India, Tiruchipally, January 1956* (Madras: CLS, 1956), 12-14.

but also in Indian understanding.[151] Devanandan, in the likeness of Jones' approach, felt the need for Christians to be in dialogue with people of other faiths.[152] Richard Taylor mentions the time he and Devanandan journeyed to the North of India during Devanandan's preparation for dialogue, and their chance meeting with a Hindu priest who had previously attended Jones' conferences.[153] This could have been an opportunity for Devanandan to look into a wider opening for interreligious dialogue although Devananadan does not mention Jones in his quest for preparation of dialogue. Robin Boyd also mentions that Devanandan did not acquaint himself with people who had made considerable efforts when he began his preparation for dialogue.[154] Above all, Jones and Devanandan, in their interpretation of Christianity centred upon Christ.

Having looked at the impact of Jones in India, especially to Indian Christian theology, his influences are visible, but are surprisingly minimal given his reputation and acceptance in India. Yet, looking back at his thought, he has a contribution to make to Indian Christian theology in general and Indian interpretation of Christ in particular.

---

151 P. D. Devanandan, *Preparation for Dialogue* (Bangalore: CISRS, 1964), 175.

152 Devanandan, *Preparation for Dialogue*, 176.

153 Taylor, *Contributions of Stanley Jones*, 10.

154 Robin Boyd, *Indian Christian Theology* (Madras: CLS, 1969), 202.

Chapter 6

Conclusion

Having looked at the various aspects of the Christ of the Indian Road, i.e., its conception, meaning, content and objectives, it is a necessity to analyse his objective to make a conclusive statement about the Christ of the Indian Road. As mentioned earlier, Jones took a different path from the way American Methodist missionaries worked in India by concentrating to evangelise the intellectual elite which Jones finds is the key of evangelise the whole of India. For they are ones who think, and that changing their mind would automatically change the minds of the people down to the lower class.[155] In attempting thus, he was in close contact with Gandhi whom he finds was the key a getting the attention of the intellectual class. Gandhi had already done the work of introducing Christ to the people of India, especially the intellectual class in his role as an ardent nationalist. Hence, it was Jones' objective to convert Gandhi to Christianity although the objective was met with failure. In addition, Jones initiated meetings with the intellectual class of India in various cities with an open objective of bringing them to Christ, for which

155 Quoted in Graham, *Extraordinary Man*, 111.

he uses the oft-mentioned 'Christ of Experience'. This openness was the distinctiveness of Jones' approach that he did not feel the need to have nothing hidden to those whom he addressed. He clearly enunciates, 'be absolutely frank-there should be no camouflage in hiding one's meaning or purpose by non-committal subjects, the audience must know exactly what it is coming to hear.'[156]

Jones' openness in his approach of communicating the message of Christ to the intellectual class of the Indian society in his dialogue with people of different religions puts Christ at the centre. For this, Richard Taylor blames Jones of being triumphalistic. [157] However, as an evangelist with an objective of attempting to bring the intellectual elite of his time to Christ, openly presenting Christ was not triumphalistic but shows his evangelistic concern. Moreover, Jones' honest and sincere approach did not repulse those who attended his meetings altogether. In fact, Martin cites that there were sometimes thousands who throng Jones' public meeting apart from those who accepted invitation to attend the Round Table Conferences.[158] This openness can be attributed to the success of Jones' dialogue with people of different religions, a dialogue which was far ahead of its time.

Stanley Jones' "Christ of the Indian Road" has another distinctive feature seen from the analysis made in the earlier chapter. The context in which it was conceived was among the intellectuals of Jones' time. Though it was presented to the intellectual class, its content and message is not a product of high academic deliberations as has been examined. To put in simple term, "Christ of the Indian Road" was an interpretation of Jesus which could be understood by all. This elemental characteristic has an important contribution to make in Indian Christian theology in that it was not sansritic and academic as opposed to the existing interpretation of Christ in India, offering a people oriented interpretation of Christ.

---

156 Jones, *Indian Road*, 32.

157 Taylor, "E. Stanley Jones," 342.

158 Martin, "Walking the Indian Road", Position Paper Number 87. The events and venues of the meetings have also been listed by Taylor. See, Taylor, *Contributions of E. Stanley Jones*, 3.

Jones "Christ of the Indian Road" has a certain objective of naturalizing Christ in India. In attempting to reach that objective, Jones has achieved a remarkable success. Jones achieves what M.M. Thomas calls a 'situational' theology in that "Christ of the Indian Road" is 'recognised and interpreted in the light of Jesus of Nazareth, that is, Christ incarnate in another situation.'[159] For Jones, Christ of the Indian Road is not different from Christ of the Galilee, except that India replaces Galilee. Jones' Christ of the Indian Road is in compliance with Thomas' finding regarding the task of Indian Christian theology:

> If the context of Indian Christian theology is the dialogue between Christ and India, the Indian Church should be prepared to look for theological insights both in the Church as she seeks to confess the faith among the peoples and cultures of India, and outside the Church among those who grapple with the truth and meaning of the Person of Christ.[160]

At this juncture, it is appropriate to state that Jones' Christ of the Indian Road, apart from achieving the status of a living theology, also attains another elemental characteristic. That Christ of the Indian Road was fruitful in helping to understand the Person of Christ, which Jones interpreted through the Cross and atonement as can be seen in the third chapter of this study.

A pertinent question that needs to be raised here is whether Stanley Jones achieves 'Indianness' in his attempt at naturalizing Christ in India. In raising this issue, it is appropriate to mention that the 'Indianness of a Christology in India does not depend upon the use of certain Sanskrit words familiar in Indian philosophy and religion,' nor does one prove its 'Indianess' by excluding all references to theological works in the West and by refusing to enter into serious dialogue with them.'[161] In this sense, Jones has arrived at some success

---

159 Thomas, *Acknowledged Christ*, 306.

160 Thomas, *Acknowledged Christ*, 316.

161 Stanley J. Samartha, *The Hindu Response to the Unbound Christ* (Madras: Christian Literature Society, 1974), 145.

in that he does not use Sanskrit words although he was not very keen in observing the second point. Yet, Jones' Christ of the Indian Road was not a direct refusal to inter into dialogue with theological works in the West, but was rather insistent in keeping Christ unbound to any particular situation, a point which Samartha concludes his analysis of the Christological task in India.[162] In addition, just as Samartha points out, Jones' Christ of the Indian Road was involved in human situations. But, Samartha does not however attempt a people centred interpretation of the Person of Christ, but goes back into the exclusive circle of interpreting Christ through Advaitic philosophy, an interpretation not understood by all people. The attempt is however made by Jones by interpreting Christ in a way which can be understood by those treading the Indian Road. In this way, Jones attains the 'purpose of Indian interpretation of Christ which is not to create an Indian theology but to communicate the message of Christ.'[163] In doing this, Jones has made a remarkable contribution to Indian interpretation of Christ and Indian theology by effectively communicating the message of Christ to the Indian people. The critique of S. K. George on Jones is that although Jones was one of the 'many apologist and exponents of Indian Christianity, yet, the *Christ of the Indian Road* was a foreign conception with the language of consolidation.'[164] But, looking at S. K. George's remark attentively, it was made on Jones' book with the same title, and not Jones' interpretation of Christ.

Jones did not attempt to construct a Christology in a strict theological sense; he only interpreted Christ in Indian terms, to his own advantage. This raises questions concerning his evangelistic motives especially if one was to use his approach in 21st century Indian theology with the looming controversy of conversion. This also becomes also an issue in an interreligious dialogue where sensitivity is shown to the integrity of different religions and their claims. Moreover, in most of his writings, Jones leaves out important

162 See Samartha, *Hindu Response*, 200.

163 "Editorial: The Christological Task in Indian" in Richard W. Taylor (Ed.), *Religion and Society: The First Twenty-Five Years 1953-1978* (Madras: CLS, 1982), 125.

164 S. K. George, *Gandhi's Challenge to Christianity* (London: George Allen & Unwin, 1939), 11.

facts and figures such as events, dates and names. This brings in the difficulty of assessing his impact, and at times the authenticity of various comments he quotes in his written works since he uses terms like a Hindu young man, a leading man of a city, a nationalist, a Vedantist etc. In addition, he does not present much of his case systematically and does not often cite the references of works quoted. He was more of a story-teller than a serious academic theologian. Bundy refers to him as a 'folk theologian, whose vision of Christian life developed through the telling and retelling of stories and experiences as well as through his sensitive involvement with a wide variety of people of diverse backgrounds.'[165]

Jones' unique approach altogether can be understood from his own words:

> There is a beautiful Indian marriage custom that dimly illustrates our task in India, and where it ends. At the wedding ceremony the women friends of the bride accompany her with music to the home of the bridegroom. They usher her into the presence of the bridegroom – that is as far as they can go, then they retire and leave her with her husband. That is our joyous task in India; to know him, to introduce him, to retire – not necessarily geographically, but to trust India with the Christ and trust Christ with India. We can only go so far- he and India must go the rest of the way.[166]

In saying this, Jones is worthy of giving recognition. He does not try to enforce his interpretation of Christ as the only way of interpreting Christ in India. His efforts and approach shows that Indians can interpret Christ in their own terms, and that Christ can be at home in India. For this concern and approach, Jones' Christ of the Indian Road can be an insight and a further challenge of interpreting Christ in simple and effective ways, not academic or sanskritic, but in terms which can be understood by those toiling and walking the Indian road.

---

165 Bundy, "The Theology of the Kingdom of God in E. Stanley Jones," 59.

166 Jones, *Indian Road*, 253-254.

Bibliography

Primary Source

Jones, E. Stanley. "Christian Missions Not Domination, not Denomination, but Christ" in *The Indian Witness*, April 3, 1934, 2.

Jones, E. Stanley. "Influence of the Indian Heritage upon Christianity" in Richard W. Taylor, *The Contribution of E. Stanley Jones*. Madras: CLS, 1973.

Jones, E. Stanley. "My Position Restated" in *Indian Witness*, 11th April, 1940, 233.

Jones, E. Stanley. "Opportunities for the Indian Church Facing Indian Nationalism" in *The Indian Witness*, August 1, 1946, 1.

Jones, E. Stanley. "Opportunities for the Indian Church Facing Indian Nationalism II" in *The Indian Witness*, August 15, 1946, 1.

Jones, E. Stanley. *Along the Indian Road*. New York: Abingdon Press, 1939.

Jones, E. Stanley. *Christ at the Round Table*. London: Hodder and Stoughton, 1928.

Jones, E. Stanley. *Mahatma Gandhi: An Interpretation*. Nashville: Abingdon-Cokesbury Press, 1948.

Jones, E. Stanley. *Songs of Ascents: A Spiritual Autobiography*. Nashville: Abingdon Press, 1968.

Jones, E. Stanley. *The Christ of the Indian Road.* London: Hodder and Stoughton, 1925.

Secondary Source

Andrews, C. F. *The Renaissance in India: Its Missionary Impact.* Edinburgh: Foreign Mission Committee of the Church of Scotland, 1912.

Ariarajah, S. Wesley "Some Glimpses into the Theology of Dr. Stanley Samartha" in C. D. Jathanna (Ed.). *Dialogue in Community: Essays in Honour of S. J. Samartha.* Mangalore: Karnataka Theological Research Institute, 1982, 231-233.

Ariarajah, S. Wesley. "Interfaith Dialogue (Dialogue, Interfaith)" in Nicholas Lossky et. al (Eds.) *Dictionary of the Ecumenical Movement.* Geneva: WCC Publications, 2002, 311-317.

Ariarajah, S. Wesley. *Hindus and Christians: A Century of Protestant Ecumenical Thought.* Grand Rapids, Michigan: Wm. B. Eerdmans, 1991.

Asirvatham, Eddy. *The Evolution of my Social Thinking.* Madras: Christian Literature Society, 1970.

Bacon, Leonard Woolsey. *A History of American Christianity.* New York: Christian Literature Company, 1897.

Boyd, R. H. S. *An Introduction to Indian Christian Theology.* Madras: Christian Literature Society, 1969.

Brown, Judith M. *Gandhi: Prisoner of Hope.* Yale: Yale University Press, 1989.

Bundy, David. "The Theology of the Kingdom of God in E. Stanley Jones" in *Wesleyan Theological Journal,* Vol. 23, No. 1 (Spring, 1988), 58-80.

Chatterjee, Margareth. *Gandhi's Religious Thought.* London: MacMillan Press, 1983.

Copplestone, J. Tremayne. *The Methodist Episcopal Church, 1896-1939/Vol. IV: Twentieth Century Perspectives.* New York: Board of Global Ministries and United Methodist Church, 1973.

Deminger, Sigfrid. *Evangelist pa Indiska Villkor: Stanley Jones och den Indiska Renassansen 1918-1930.* Orebro: Bokforlaget Libris, 1985.

Devanandan, P. D. *Preparation for Dialogue.* Bangalore: CISRS, 1964.

Devanandan, P. D. "The India We Live In" in *Presenting Christ to India Today: Three Addresses and a Sermon delivered to the Synod of The Church of South India, Tiruchipally, January 1956.* Madras: CLS, 1956), 1-26.

Devanandan, P. D. *Christian Concern in Hinduism.* Bangalore: CISRS, 1961.

Devanesen, Chandran. *The Infinite Christ.* Madras: Christian Literature Society, 1948.

Dieter, Melvin E. *The Holiness Revival of the Nineteenth Century.* Lanham: The Scarecrow Press, 1996.

England, John C. et. al. (Eds.). *Asian Christian Theologies: A Research Guide to Authors, Movement, Sources,* Vol. I. New York: Orbis Books, 2002.

Farquhar, John Nicols. *The Crown of Hinduism.* London: Oxford University Press, 1913.

Fisher, Luis. *The Life of Mahatma Gandhi.* London: Jonathan Cape, 1951.

Fleming, Daniel Johnson. *Each with His Own Brush: Contemporary Christian Art in Asia and Africa.* Nashville: Friendship Press, 1938.

Frykenberg, Robert Eric. "Christians in India: An Historical Overview of their Complex Origins" in Robert Eric Frykenberg (Ed.). *Christians and Missionaries in India: Cross Cultural Communication since 1500 with Special Reference to Caste, Conversion, and Colonialism.* Cambridge: William B Eerdmans, 2003, 33-61.

George, S. K. *Gandhi's Challenge to Christianity.* London: George Allen & Unwin, 1939.

Graham, Stephen A. *Ordinary Man, Extraordinary Mission: The Life and Work of E. Stanley Jones*. Nashville: Abingdon Press, 2005.

Martin, Paul A. J. *Missionary of the Indian Road: A Theology of Stanley Jones*. Bangalore: Theological Book Trust, 1996.

Martin, Paul A.J. "Walking the Indian Road: The Contribution of E. Stanley Jones to Missionary Theology in India" in *Collected Papers of North Atlantic Missiology Project and Currents in World Christianity Project 1996-2001*. CD ROM, Position Paper Number 87.

Mathews, James K. *South of the Himalayas: One Hundred Years of Methodism in India and Pakistan*. Nashville: Editorial Department, Board of Missions of the Methodist Church, 1955.

Mayhew, A. I. "The Christian Ethic and India" in L. S. S. O'Malley (Ed.). *Modern India and the West: A Study of the Interaction of their Civilizations*. London: Oxford University Press, 1941, 319-320.

Narayan, Shriman (Ed.). *The Selected Works of Mahatma Gandhi*, Vol. VI. Ahmedabad: Navajivan Publishing House, 1968.

Narayan, Shriman (Ed.). *The Selected Works of Mahatma Gandhi*, Vol. I. Ahmedabad: Navajivan Publishing House, 1968.

Paranjoti, Violet. *As Evangelist on the Indian Scene: Dr. E. Stanley Jones*. Bombay: Bombay Book & Tract Society, 1970.

Peters, John L. *Christian Perfection and American Methodism*. Nashville: Abingdon Press, 1956.

Pierson, Paul E. "The Student Volunteer Movement for Foreign Missions (SVM)" in A. Scott Moreau (Ed.). *Evangelical Dictionary of World Missions*. Grand Rapids: Baker Books, 2000, 914.

Radhakrishnan, S (Ed.). *Mahatma Gandhi: Essays and Reflections on his Life and Work*. London: George Allen & Unwin, 1939.

Rajamani, A. Noble. "Mr. Evangelist" in Violet Paranjoti, *As Evangelist on the Indian Scene: Dr. E. Stanley Jones*. Bombay: Bombay Book & Tract Society, 1970, 109-112.

Rao, K. L. Sheshagiri. *Mahatma Gandhi and Comparative Religion*. Delhi: Motilal Banarsidass, 1978.

Richards, Glyn. *The Philosophy of Gandhi: A Study of his Basic Ideas.* London: Curzon Press, 1982.

Samartha, Stanley J. "Dialogue as a Continuing Christian Concern" *The Ecumenical Review* , Vol. 23, No. 2, April 1971, 129-142.

Samartha, Stanley J. "Dialogue: Significant Issues in the Continuing Debate" in *The Ecumenical Review*, Vol. 24, No. 3, July 1972, 327-340.

Samartha, Stanley J. "Guidelines on Dialogue" in *The Ecumenical Review*, Vol. 31, No. 2, April 1979, 155-161.

Samartha, Stanley J. "The Progress and Promise of Inter-faith Dialogue," in *Journal of Ecumenical Studies*, Vol. 9, No. 3, 1972, 463-476.

Samartha, Stanley J. *The Hindu Response to the Unbound Christ.* Madras: Christian Literature Society, 1974.

Synan, Vinson. *The Holiness-Pentecostal Movement in the United States.* Grand Rapids: Wm B. Eerdmans, 1971.

Takenaka, Masao "Review of Jesus in Indian Paintings by Richard W. Taylor" in *The Ecumenical Review*, Vol. 29, No. 1, January 1977, 102-103.

Takenaka, Masao. *Christian Art in Asia.* Tokyo: Kyo Bun Kwan and CCA, 1975.

Taylor, Richard W. "Some Interpretations of Jesus in Indian Painting" in Saral K. Chatterjee (introduced.), *Acknowledging the Lordship of Christ: Selected Writings of Richard W. Taylor.* Delhi: ISPCK, 1992, 1-31.

Taylor, Richard W. "E. Stanley Jones 1884-1973: Following the Christ of the Indian Road" in Gerald H. Anderson, Robert T. Coote, Norman A. Horner and James M. Phillips (Eds.). *Mission Legacies: Biographical Studies of Leaders of the Modern Missionary Movement.* Maryknoll: Orbis Books, 1994, 339-347.

Taylor, Richard W. "Editorial: The Christological Task in Indian" in Richard W. Taylor (Ed.). *Religion and Society: The First Twenty-Five Years 1953-1978.* Madras: Christian Literature Society, 1982, 121-126.

Taylor, Richard W. *Jesus in Indian Paintings*. Madras: Christian Literature Society, 1975.

Thomas, M. M. *The Acknowledged Christ of the Indian Renaissance*. London: SCM Press, 1969.

Thomas, M. M. & T. K. Thomas. "Preface" in P. T. Thomas, *The Theology of Chakkarai with Selections from his Writings*. Bangalore: CISRS, 1968, iii-v.

Thomas, T. K. *The Witness of S. K. George*. Madras: Christian Literature Society, 1970.

Walls, Andrew F. *The Missionary Movement in Christian History: Studies in the Transmission of Faith*. Edinburgh: T & T Clark, 1996.

Whitehead, Henry. *Indian Problems in Religion Education Politics*. London: Constable & Co., 1924.

Internet Source

http://www.storyofpakistan.com/articletext.asp?artid=A120

http://www.mcc.edu.in/index.php?Itemid=56&id=30&option=com_content&task=view

http://www.wcc-coe.org/wccnews/07-english.html

Index

D

E

F

G

H

I